Steveston

Steveston

poems
DAPHNE MARLATT

photographs
ROBERT MINDEN

RONSDALE PRESS

RONSDALE PRESS
3350 West 21st Avenue
Vancouver, B.C., Canada
V6S 1G7

Set in Perpetua: 12.5 pt on 14
Typesetting: Julie Cochrane
Printed in China
Cover Photograph: Robert Minden, *Hideo (Henry) Kokubo,* 1974
Cover Design: Julie Cochrane
Back Cover Photo Credit for Robert Minden: Nancy Walker (1998)
Back Cover Photo Credit for Daphne Marlatt: John Reeves (1999)

Ronsdale Press wishes to thank the Canada Council for the Arts, the Government of Canada through the Book Publishing Industry Development Program (BPIDP), and the Province of British Columbia through the British Columbia Arts Council for their support of its publishing program.

The first edition of *Steveston* was published by Talonbooks in 1974;
the second edition by Longspoon Press in 1984.

CANADIAN CATALOGUING IN PUBLICATION DATA

Marlatt, Daphne, 1942–
    Steveston

    ISBN 0-921870-80-9

    1. Steveston (B.C.) — Poetry.   2. Japanese Canadians — British
Columbia — Steveston — Poetry.   3. Steveston (B.C.) — Pictorial works.
I. Minden, Robert. II. Title.
PS8576.A74S7 2001   C811'.54   C00-911141-7
PR9199.3.M36S8 2001

For their time, their stories, their interest and kindness, our thanks go to:

Henry Kokubo, Koko Johnson, Inez and Charlie Huovinen, Unosuke Sakamoto, Spud Matsushita, Buck Suzuki, Rintaro Hayashi, Maya Koizumi, Andy Anderson and his staff at the Richmond Art Center.

We are grateful also for the evocative work of those early photographers of Steveston: Philip Timms and F. Dundas Todd.

"seeking to perceive it as it stands . . ."

JAMES AGEE

Imagine: a town

Imagine a town running

                (smoothly?
a town running before a fire
canneries burning

          (do you see the shadow of charred stilts
on cool water? do you see enigmatic chance standing
just under the beam?

             He said they were playing cards in the
Chinese mess hall, he said it was dark (a hall? a shack.
they were all, crowded together on top of each other.
He said somebody accidentally knocked the oil lamp over, off
the edge

       where stilts are standing, Over the edge of the
dyke a river pours, uncalled for, unending:

                where chance lurks
fishlike, shadows the underside of pilings, calling up his hall
the bodies of men & fish corpse piled on top of each other (residue
time is, the delta) rot, an endless waste the trucks of production

grind to juice, driving thru

                      smears, blood smears in the dark
dirt) this marshland silt no graveyard can exist in but water swills,
endlessly out of itself to the mouth

                         ringed with residue, where
chance flicks his tail & swims, thru

Imperial Cannery, 1913

Standing inside the door (the river . . .) how shadow lies
just inside the cannery floor, sun, pouring down outside,
the river streaming slow, slow, by. Now she feels old enough,
now she is wearing her long print dress & leaning into the
threshold, waiting for work, the wheel that time is, Whose hands
are standing still, hers, empty, Whose friends also surround her,
waiting, waiting all morning for the fish to come. Nothing moves
but occasional strands of long hair the subtle wind is lifting,
up off the river, the Fraser, mouth of the Fraser here where it
debouches, into marsh, delta, swirling around & past those
pilings of the cannery wharf they are standing on, muddy &
pale grey teeming, invisible fish . . .

                         Now she is old enough to be her
mother inside, working, with the smallest one standing by her skirt
in grubby dress, & the blood streams down the wooden cutting board
as the "iron chink" (that's what they call it) beheads each fish . . .

Now she is old enough for the wheel's turn, she is feeling her
body in its light dress wind blows thru, as past the faces of
her friends, likewise silent, impassive. Wind blows thru

those open doors (two) because, in the dark where machines are,
& the cans, & the steam, & a cavern of men with rolled up
sleeves & straw hats, & men in oilcloth slickers spattered with
fish gut, beyond & across the corner of that dark stands
another door, & the sail of a boat crossing the river, wind,
wind . . . An open door, where men unload their hauls of fish, the
collector's boat, float, sliding one, a hundred, on top of another,
their own scale grease that keeps them alive in sea they're
taken from to dry, in open sun on an open dock.

                                            But she is in her
element, dreaming of sails, her father's, or a friend's son, at the
Imperial which owns their boat, their net, their debt. But the
Fraser gives of itself, incessantly, rich (so the dream goes),
& wooden houses jammed on pilings close together, leaning, with
wooden walks & muddy alleys, laundry, & the dry marsh grass that
stutters out of silt the dykes retain, from a flowing
ever eroding & running river . . .

dreaming, of fabric she saw at Walker's Emporium, & the ribbon. A
woman of means she dreams, barefoot on the dock in the wind, leaning
into her threshold of work, machines, the wheel that keeps turning
turning, out of its wooden sleeve, the blade with teeth marked:
for marriage, for birth, for death.

Pour, pour

                    from its bank) this river is rivering urgency, roar
(goku, goku) thru any hole, like boats race tide a millrace, as,
the possible entry of this channel for, invisible under their hulls
& flying heels, the fish re-enter time, racing north of Roberts Bank
past Albion Dyke, then Woodward Reach opposite Woodward Landing
(where the ferry ran) by Woodward Slough, then Gravesend Reach &
City Reach the river proper lies, past any tidal reach (renew) fish
seek their source, which is, their proper place to die . . .

                                    "This river is
alive," he says, crippled fisherman on the radio watching water
swollen with filth, with sewage, milldirt, strain at the sandbag
dyke, at its container, uncontainable, irrational (hence renewable)
creature, swelling up & birthing, huge, past all their plans & plants,
its urgency to meet the sea where men go, when they are able, like the
fish. It eddies too, backwater Hong Wo, where (unable) moss
shackles an abandoned roof, or marsh grass thick with seed heads
silent (bunkhouse) into a wind live off the river sun is scouring,
walk, a wall will be, silent as light-rimmed wood, knowing what?
evidence?

gaunt, a face glimpsed from behind tatter windowhanging
keeps, he keeps their store (his, haunt) locked dust, its stilled clock
barely visible, shelves still stocked, in part, in part vacant-eyed,
he stares trying not to be seen, to see, he is the visible remnant
of time's push, here where it eddies back on his suspicion, under the
fencedup place he keeps his dog, back of the dock, this place (source)
he haunts, his bark, or its, invisible guardian of old receipts,
accounts not rendered, months yellowing into irrelevant years (some
seven in quick succession, glancing, like light off water no one
registers, the way tide swells up under these pilings where the tag ends
of his mind keep, Hong Wo's, good luck chips, echoing down the galvanized
floor of wash tank across the way, in back of what was once, one, two,
three, four, company, source of (need as cash) or, a kind of company account
no hand skims now, closing in on this life, this, or this, foreclosed at
dusk now, opening the door he wanders out to sit, leaning his chair
against the wall & contemplating closedup house boards, a sweltering
mattress or the few remaining cards: as visages, his vision is accretion
uncountable (is he? accountable?) or facing mountains he can't see, wires,
& the roar of Richmond skyline (money), only the falsefront silhouette
'west' is occupies his mind, disused (opportune) broccoli box tide swells &
moves, this way or that, but always to cast up finally in the muck low
tide shallows, or the last spasm a visible body leaves, some seed as
imprint or, continuance, continuing to pour/down as light, or time,
this town down stream its own downpour . . .

Moon

        half moon, hot night. water seeping up, wetting
island dirt. It's river, rank odour of river mud banks, the
strait, the sea. That smell of night come lightly on the body of
the earth's heat, full of the day.

                        It's stagnant ditch water, drainage
gathering scum, Lulu Island, dyked off from the sea.

                                Half moon,
Saturday night, hot June: already would have shot the season in
all up & down her banks a sound of cedar corks crescending
over the gunnels of boats, paid out by hand, at six, on Sunday night,
the week begins. Night before, ten thousand people pack the town, a
crush, on the board sidewalks' eight-foot planks, the taverns'
rustle of silk, boots. boots upstairs. pitcher of water blood hot,
heat trapt up in those gable rooms, in a gambling eye . . .

White as the moon, who was she? apart from the different dreams they
had, in smoke & whiskey, & then the Indians, Chinese, Japanese unknown
in numbered houses. But mostly those her like up from San Francisco,
turning in the aura of a silk-pleated shade those white arms
suddenly lifted, naked, Lulu. Lulu Sweet's namesake this Island,

spawning in the dive of fisherman kids under the walk for change that
spills from tight & multiple pockets of the packers, Scotch-English,
Phoenix, Colonial, Paramount, this moon-crazed industry (you hear that
splash at night of nets?), this town . . .

Now so quiet only frogs sing in ditches soon to be covered as per
housing development, each internal room focused on a further internal
screen, whose smaller & smaller ponds of thought these "channels"
bring

      In from the Outside, where the night lives, this spring, this
moon as every spring: freshet, & the salmon churning black waters,
darker depths.

        A few people drink in the Steveston, a few
young men: stopt up, burning, slow, nowhere to go, no crowds to
light, no strange women, no gambling games, no risk. Except the
occasional storm outside, the rare failure of guaranteed equipment,
the unexplained accident

        as shipwreck, or, only the *smaller* packers
forced out, bought up.

        This corporate growth that monopolizes
the sun. moon & tide, fish-run. So they see nothing remarkable
in this, they know it like the back of their hands on a familiar
table, like fish conveyed by belt to the steady chopping of steel
blades. Beer to lips, end of a shift, end of another week. It
sucks them dry, these men soaking in their beer (so many thousand
cans today), these women in white, tired or wearily hopeful, drained
by the ditches of their unsatisfied lives.

Steveston as you find it:

                      multiplicity simply there: the physical matter of
the place (what matters) meaning, don't get theoretical now, the cannery.

It's been raining, or it's wet. Shines everywhere a slick on the surface of
things wet gumboots walk over, fish heads & other remnants of sub/ or
marine life, brought up from under. Reduced to the status of things hands
lop the fins off, behead, tail, tossed, this matter that doesn't matter,
into a vat or more correctly box the forklifts will move, where they swim,
flat of eye — deathless that meaningless stare, "fisheye" (is it only
dead we recognize them?) in a crimson sauce of their own blood.

                                    We orient
always toward the head, & eyes (yes) as knowing, & knowing us, or what we do.
But these, this, is "harvest." These are the subhuman facets of life we the
town (& all that is urban, urbane, our glittering table service, our white
wine, the sauces we pickle it with, or ourselves), live off. These torsos.
& we throw the heads away. Or a truck passes by, loaded with offal for what
we also raise to kill, mink up the valley.

                          That's not it. It's wet,
& there's a fish smell. There's a subhuman, sub/marine aura to things. The
cavernous "fresh fish" shed filled with water, with wet bodies of dead fish,

in thousands, wet aprons & gloves of warm bodies whose hands expertly trim, cut, fillet, pack these bodies reduced to non-bodies, nonsensate food *these* bodies ache from, feet in gumboots on wet cement, arms moving, hands, cold blowing in from open doors facing the river, whose ears dull from, the insensate noise of machinery, of forklifts, of grinding & washing, of conveyor belt. Put on an extra sweater, wear long underwear against the damp that creeps up from this asphalt, from this death that must be kept cool, fresh.

"DISINFECT YOUR GLOVES BEFORE RESUMING WORK."

That no other corpus work within it. Kept at the freshest, at the very point of mutable life, diverting, into death. To be steamed in cans, or baked, frozen in fillets, packaged sterile for the bacteria of living bodies to assimilate. break down. Pacific Ocean flesh.

No, that's not it. There's a dailiness these lives revolve around, also immersed. Shifts, from seven to four or otherwise. Half an hour for lunch. & a long paperwrapt & tied form outside the lunchroom, keeping cool. 'til shift's end & the fridge, supper, bed. "my life," etc.

"You leave 2 minutes after 4, & not before, you understand? Two minutes after." Two minutes, as if that, together with the sardine cans for ashtray, made all the difference. Which is, simply, as two Japanese women sit, relaxing with their fifteen minute coffee out of thermos, more likely hot soup, one rearranges the chrysanthemums, red & yellow, she placed in an empty can on their table this morning when the day began. Or more directly how in "fresh fish" the lunchrooms, men's & women's, face over an expanse of roof with flowerboxes even, river & the delta, Ladner, space. & remain spacious, time turned calendar of kimona'd beauty, kneeling, on the wall. While in the cannery close to wharfedge they face north, backed by old wooden lockers to the door: DO NOT SPIT IN THE GARBAGE. USE THE TOILETS. & here they flood in together, giggling, rummaging thru bags, eating grapes, girlish even ("I've worked here 20 years") under severe green kerchief like Italian peasants, except that they are mostly Japanese, plunked under a delicate mobile of Japanese ribbon fish in their gumboots & socks. Break, from routine, with the ease of tired bodies laughing, for what? "It's life." *Their* life?

                                             Or how the plant packs their lives, chopping
off the hours, contains *them* as it contains first aid, toilets, beds, the
vestige of a self-contained life in this small house back of the carpentry
shed, where two woodburners are littered with pots & hot plates, & the table
still bears its current pattern of dominoes. Where a nude on the wall glints
kittenish at one of the two small rooms inside, each with iron bed. Some
sleeping place between shifts? Dark. Housing wet dreams, pale beside the
clank of forklift, supply truck, welding shed.

It's a mis-step, this quiet gap on everyone else's shift, when you're off,
when accidental gravel rattles loud on the wooden walk. wan sun. coffee,
gone cold. There's a surface skin of the familiar, familial. Running into
shadow, where old socks, someone else's intimate things, call up the fishy
odour of cunt, of lamp black in the old days you could hear them screwing
behind their door (cardboard), & even the kitchen still exists to pull you
back in, to smallness, a smell of coal, the aura of oil, of what comes up
from under, sleeping — nets, wet still from riverbottom, & the fish.

This darker seam that slips underneath the coppery gleam of all those cans stacked
flat after flat, waiting transfer. Men. & Women. Empty familiar lunchroom,
& the dream, pounding with the pound of machinery under mountains of empty
packer pens at night, the endless (white) stream of flesh passing under the knives,
To be given up, gone, in a great bleeding jet, into that other (working) world.

How it goes

Men sleeping, lives, or lives sleeping, doors. On Moncton, in the
store window, a pall draped placard reads:

> In Memoriam
> Steveston Post Office
> Doors closed
> May 13th 1972

Women wend their way past, if they do,
unconcerned (it flows) or crossing doors, grocery, cannery, library floors,
"you can't hear yourself think with all that noise," "they're tearing up the
pavement on Number One again." They continue, as if. it wasn't so long ago
they changed direction, roads, leaving sea & moving inland, inroads to a
heart that changes. Monopoly. "The kids grow up & go elsewhere," she said,
not fishing, not limited to that, or limited, how the company pays, & she
stays. Somewhere, children keep growing up baseball heroes, while sun slowly
lightens the doctor's floor, behind blinds, behind history, a facade
salvaged & rendered useful, or the old houses back of Steves place,
shacks groaning awry in wind, into cow muck, into canary grass . . .

the slap slap continues as a clock ticks somewhere on Moncton
& she comes home to the empty house . . .

May day May day May day. He called Pan.
She should have cut the grass. Yesterday. He shouldn't have painted the house.
Yesterday. Yesterday was fine. & now the demolition crew, a church radio
floating off somewhere in the blue, while morning, eternal morning twines
weed, bindweed, creeps in the empty door at noon. At noon, "maybe get a few
hours rest," they said, they sent her home.

        "Distress." How it continues.
Maybe it was, she thinks, maybe it might have been, a packer leaving the
Gulf Oil barge, crowd of fish boxes, silver, riding the sun. late afternoon,
8 men. 7 to help. They said he could . . . Or later, "you can sleep
all the way up to Bull Harbour if you want," his chipt blue mug sliding
across the cabin floor, but, the way he wore his shirt, collar up against those
small hairs of his back, twisted somehow, stooped. They knew. Riding waves
or rising, into them, to the occasion. Heroism is not confined to the
sea. A pain, a pain rising & no one . . .

"Distress signal should not be used where Urgency signal will do." & so,
mouth shut, silent, falling into the sea — why won't they cry out? Doors
close. & she is haunted by it, as she crosses, into shadow, any silent
sunny street.

Sea Trek etc

           trickle of broken hose. old netting, sacking, rope.
paint everywhere. penboards on end & painted silver. poles with
bells to be fitted, new springs & line. the sound of a boat
rubbing against tire, whisper of rope, shift across rope as a
boat lifts or falls.

           Sea Trek, Elma K, Miss Nikko 70, ready,
day after day copper painted & caulked & overhauled, now they
wait, feeling that suck in green & oily shallows, feeling
afternoon leaf so close at hand, & late (derisive, cluck of a
gull domestic, finally) they wait, for headway out to the open
seas/ the open season, current, storm: & fish.

Low Tide. A beached vessel,

                                    small grey gillnetter, chained to the
dock so close in to shore she's high & dry on rocks, angularly
beached, bleached, like some dying fish.

                                    Where nothing belongs
in all this absent morning, only sun who owns these shells of
cannery housing, these unused footbridges, these brambles whose fruit
no one picks. Silent boats. Docks serving only sun, & wind off the
open waters. Moving. Down the track come 3 boys idle, looking for
some — Wow, a boat.

                                    Her sullen cabin's locked, but two of them
violate a side window. Hey a searchlight! Does it work? Look at
this! An empty bottle, flung in glittering arc across the sun,
smashes into a thousand bits.

The third, jimmying her door, Hey you guys, is there a metal
pipe in there? If you find a metal pipe I could smash every door
in the place.

                                    The place? These kids, who live by the sea & know
nothing of boats. But orders, orders of power, of hoarded wealth.

Insistent, hey you guys, to break in on what the others are earnestly
engaged in: Somebody's pants! Got any money? Look, batteries,
gasoline, a licence — I could be a driver of a boat. Hey, cool!
this is a masterkey you know, it'll open up that door.

Inscrutably closed, she allows no keys to hold, nothing so easy —
as the fear somebody's beating somebody to it, every minute:
Hold this, hurry, I can rip the door off.

An older man, who's
walking down the tracks toward the Esso dock, anonymously watching,
stops at that. With voice of authority: Boys, you're not supposed
to be on there!

Sudden pause. Not on this boat?

No sir, not on any boat. Silence while they try it on for size,
unwilling. If the patrolman comes along you'll be in trouble.
Then he, unwilling to meet their eyes, walks off.

There's a lull, like a momentary cloud, an anxious thought. Is that
the patrol boat? Naaw, he's kidding. Come on!

Back to the joyous act of "making" her, their secret catch.

End of Cannery Channel

Trolling bells, hammering. A storm of bells as the hammering
increases. Bird song. Grass smell. On the floats a litter
of corks, paint, packing cases, rags, freshly painted pen boards.
Tatters of net. raindrenched to the dock. And, at the end,
a clean looking troller, starboard pole dropped flat. Two men
bent over, replacing rusty springs & talking with a third who's
looking on. Who glances at my notebook.

"Are you going to raise that pole? I'd like to watch."

"She wants to watch! (Laughing, he says something in Japanese
to the other two.) You gonna *help?*"

"Sure. I'll help you."

"I'm kidding. These are heavy poles."

"How heavy?"

"Well, flat on the wharf she's 200 pounds easy. Once you get her
to a 45 degree angle one man can lift, but down she takes 3 men."

Water laps softly against the hull. There's a curious backwater
stillness to their work.

"Hot day huh? You want something to drink? (The others laugh.)
You wanna beer? We give you beer & maybe you dance for us eh?
Charlie get her a drink."

"No, no I don't dance." The older man offers a sunwarm coke,
simply, as if disregarding the other's comments. "Thanks."
& goes back to his work. "Those springs are for the bells?
when you get a bite?"

He's leaning against the sawhorse wondering what I want. "Yeah, sure,
you married?"

"No."

"Hippie?"

"No. Why?"

"Why not? Hippie's okay. Take me, I work hard & then go home to
the same old pork chop every night, you know what I mean? But you,
you have variety. Turkey one night, beef the next. Maybe try a
little fish eh?" (nudging the others)

I'm clearly a woman on their float. Too weak to lift the pole,
old enough to have tastes — "you know what I mean?" He eyes me
across the rift of language, race, & sex. Should I go?

Laughs suddenly, calls something in Japanese. They've tightened in
the last spring. Water reflects light off the underside of the
crosspiece (white) the pole will rise into. Suddenly mobilized,
they board her. Three men pulling on ropes, heave, grunt, call.
The boat shifts under lifting weight. Higher, she's pulling in,
close to the mast. Two hold, while he climbs up & hammers the
metal brace into place, grins down:

"See what it's like?"

In time

                    how the river washes them bare, roots trees
put down, knotted & twining into the wash of the Gulf, tidal, in, in & out
to the mouth, the gulf all trees, roots, clumps & knottings of men's nets
wash out to. Washing from east to west, how the river flows, washing its
filth downstream & silting islands of work men dredge their channels thru,
grassland, sedge. The work it takes to keep men busy, dredge at it, all
day long to keep a channel thru, street, straight thru (west) to . . .

This chugging of an Easthope moving east to west, waiving sandbar, mudflat,
thru marsh you can't see past, as earlier steamer for Mrs Steves, "But ma'am
no one lives there!" To be made *here,* island of grass seen as pasturage,
dairy farm. & then an island settlement, a settlement mentality that
settles down a street that doesn't go straight thru, pacing the river's
winding edge, that says oblivious, good soil here we'll put our roots down.
And the river runs away with them, flood, storm, all manner of lost
belongings gone, anchorless on out to sea . . .

                    The edge, the edge. Settled by it. Camped rather. Cluster of
fishing shacks temporary as those Japanese who slept on boats arriving, each
season, for the fish, to stay, stray into settlement, believing still they were
only here this year, sending money home & staying on to the next, & the next,

& the natives, whose longtime summer ground this was, coming to fish, whole bands whose women & children end by working the canneries, staying in Indian tenements, & it all settles down into an order of orders, the Chinese tyee boss, & the cans hammered out by his men, orders of cash handed down thru the messhall, the gambling & fires, fire & flood.

Always on the edge of, a Gulf where the river runs. West. by East/hope, the push to "make it," that leap into the end of pain, struggle, into "settling down," finally, into cash as, security. But it continues, this westward drift. Islands of it moving west, 1000 feet per century. & this is not the end, this accumulation along the way, deposits (in a bank, in the Richmond Credit Union, in shares in BC Packers, in) a town whose main street moves, as Manoah did, from Moncton New Brunswick, west, in a vision of telephone poles, wires, cement. A straight line from east to west, from farm at its eastern end, to Steveston Hotel, knife in teeth, Canada Fish.

Shadowy, this piratical emblem of another era. Boomtown. Dream of seizing silver wealth that swims, & fixing it in solid ground, land, home. A mis-reading of the river's push. Now Moncton Street walks a straight line that begins & ends. Never a river, not even at season's peak or its end, tho it returns, at moments of, it begins & ends, the day. The school day for instance when they stand in 2's & 3's with bicycles by the Marine Grocery. At times Christine's cafe is almost full & the hardware does a running business, but no one runs & the street does not flow. They have coffee at certain times of the day, they meet, the fisheries officials, truckers, & men off their boats repairing, overhauling, come up to warm themselves on their way to the bank. These individual lives, discrete, closed off from one another, but known & recognized. Islands of men the day weaves its way thru. Going someplace? A store with no name, bales of net in the door. Stores for no end, the unused highball glasses no one buys. Stores begin & end, small personable lairs, "Tom's TV moved to Minamoru" up island where the tracts go — where the tracks went farms used to lie, with their strawberry pickers & cranberry bogs on fire, razed now to smoking inland freeway & North Arm plants . . .

Is there a gap? There is discontinuity as Moncton, cowled in its quiet normalcy, intends a straight line the health inspector's Packard drives down, & he unfolds, huge, & climbs out & crosses into Christine's. & the fishermen sit with elbows on the counter, sipping coffee & talking, or not talking, & nod. & the fisheries men greet him, & the truckers know him, & Christine who is small & not Christine, who is quiet & Chinese, smiles & brings him coffee as he packs himself, somehow, into the booth. Have you seen his brother? he has a twin, the trucker says, just as huge.

Always there is this shadow, long, that underlies the street & twins it, running it to ground. As the river, at Atlas camp, throws up sand that cuts the line Moncton extends (in mind) to the end. A line that lies, like Moncton straight ahead, ignores this shadow that wavers & wanders, collecting islands of lives, leaves them stranded or suddenly, after some years visible as, time passing, picking stucco off the wall outside Hiro's, or drinking pop & trading bubblegum cards. It lengthens slowly around them, slanting past Island Cleaners, past the Richmond pool hall, past River Radio. Puddles, clouds shining in them. So that this air of establishment, this density that is cementblock Steveston Hardware or the old brick DRUGS now L& L Discount, settles in the unseeing eyes of the old man in the pool hall, awash in beer & sentiment, into history, into what he clings to now as evidence (in time —) of "his" story.

Work

Glass of water on a hot day, at the counter. Water or sevenup.
Christine's: hotter than the street. Elbows on counter in quiet
solitude, locked into singleness the highboned profile of his face,
nevertheless like theirs flushed by the sun, declares *Fraser Princess*
tied up at floats some mile away, idle with the other boats. Now
fishing days're cut to one a week for sockeye. Thursday. Middle of
August almost.

Hello. His handshake lingers into holding-
hands — I'm pleased to see you — as he slides into the booth —
How are you? — squeezing my palm.

Last seen on the docks, fisherman of
consequence, quiet in the knowledge of his gear, his sons, their mutual
help, his years' experience here & in the world, as union executive,
salted always with their evacuation & return. The bitter seed of it
simply his protest, No I fish . . . I handled *some* of their affairs,
that's all.

Whose invisibility stalks beside him like that
second skin his boat, appropriate to his dimensions, source & home.
Despite a house furnished with cannery pay, his wife's domain. But his,

at sea a tight & familiar space that's known, the way the poles are
set, how well she handles given uncertain weather; given fuel, a reliable
engine, she'd travel to Japan & back. No, it's the force or wake she
leaves, her cut of displaced water down the channel: It's the power to
motion, to *move* . . .

               Who will insist (so are you married? no? how's this?
patting my crotch) my presence haunts the dock, for what other reason
but these fishermen who cut the water of the channel proudly with their
boats, Cut, with a powerful motion, thru the weight of all that
surrounds them, on out to sea . . .

                      Vision. Seen by them
as sexual obsession? Who, hands on the wheel, are driven by the
necessity of fishing, noise & confusion of gear, fish & the boat itself
nothing more than hard work, over & over.

                    But still, his hand pushing
down there, the teasing smile, "Next time I fish West Coast I take you
with me eh?" that persists, that isn't meant to tease but to imply . . .

                        No, it's an old
dream my hair, my body happen to fit: the incarnate goal of all
that's *out there,* given birth in crowded ghetto conditions,
necessity to work up out of that mass, the pressure always ("after
the war they wouldn't even rent a house to us") to feel what one
man can do, where he can go . . .

But then, he's 70, & they talk, the men in their coffee room on the
wharf, over dominoes & flower cards, of sex & young girls ("who's
your new girlfriend, Charlie?") of the hippies tied to government
wharf, what they'd be like, those free young ones who don't, it seems,
have to work.

              (does he see me as one of them? "Come down to my boat
Saturday — I'll give you a salmon." What can I give in return?

That I persist, also, in seeing *them,* these men,
who are cut down to one day a week: their technology too great for
the crop to bear, $600 worth in one day off one boat. The persistence
that has always in the industry characterized them. He *knows* he's an
expert fisherman, tho deprecates, "Oh one day a week's easier for an
old man like me." But idle, how strange that idleness sits on one
given to work — A glass of water, a glass of sevenup, in town, at a
cafe counter. So familiar it's boring. But for the dream that surfaces
when the young woman from *out there* walks in, with whom, momentarily,
over a hamburger & a glass of water, he connects.

"Slave of the canneries"

                        dipping into his album, fisherman's
oldest son. Beached in the mountains. Raised on fish to
fish. As young boatpuller seasick ("my dad, he used to get so
mad at me he'd dump me on the wharf," on solid ground:

Reifel Sanctuary: photos of this man with birds, geese,
tucked under one arm. Working white millionaire's ground
with care, for flood gates, trees' growth, observation tower.
Photos of the family house, the family "his" he worked for.
His also, *Lone Eagle,* must go fishing to support, age 23,
nine brothers & sisters & the grandmother whose friend ("she
knew a little bit about such things") delivered them in *this*
house on the drainage canal, company-owned, on pilings so
eaten away they have to jack it with a shingle bolt from
salvaged logs.

            Stench of rotting cannery offal floating by,
shit house seepage from these company houses crammed side by side,
footbridges they'd wheel their netcarts over, by ditches drained
by tide. Drainage of this island salvaged out of saltmarsh, these
people drained, resting in their barely salvaged houses where

rats skitter, night, eat at nets drying upstairs the hunger of
eleven people rests on:

                    grace of company loans (debt), of split
cabbage salvaged from slightly wealthier Japanese farms, "our diet —
rice, salted fish, & vegetables," day in, day out ("I still like
salted fish"), survival as the *minimum* requirement, nothing more.
hoped for. given the limits (sawmill, farm, or fish . . .

                        These mountains now,
New Denver, rise up round a slow lake windblown sometimes, seeming to
go nowhere. By Carpenter Creek, Orchard so humanly overgrown, a
ghetto for evacuees: small shacks again crammed side by side,
brown shingled this time, fronting the lake. Two thousand Japanese
in a few square blocks. Uprooted from the flats, the muddy river,
saltwind. Trucked in or departed by train to landlocked winter
where the clear air, frozen water's good for TB they say
(hemorrhaged in Hastings Park building human pens), "It was a
good experience." "How can you say that?" "For the next generation.
Look at my daughter, she's a pharmacist!"

       And so curiously pulled out of
the delta's restraining ring of debt broken by mass theft
(seizure at government level), these impoverished "enemies of
the state," transplanted & forced into new growth, shed a
mass of memoirs that evidence their real estate the four
walls testify to, over the years, room after room added, still
not finished.

       To the man who gardens, cares for
the old folks' home, caretaker of the ghetto water tower (invisible
geese under one arm), marker of past loves & past faces gone
with a river cresting, Immoveably settled here like some crustacean
in this valley where nothing runs to sea except the water, "one of
the few remaining lakes of B.C. . . . sufficiently pure & unpolluted"
to drink from / To: the pool, the still lake of our muddy &
intermingled present.

Not to be taken

                                                      from Lum Poy's back door facing due
west across an abandoned field (150 acres of good soil "assembled
& sold by Al Austin") beyond the dyke which humps hiding marsh
(you can hear visiting wild geese there), hidden, channel markers &
the jetty, only: mountains of Island visible in all that fire dusking
deeper & deeper tongues of scarlet purple grey — this Gulf pour,
into a cavernous mouth of flame & wind & water westward, ruffling skin
heat caressed by dew start underfoot, in seed grass, rank wild
water smell of

                                       River, rolling out of the darker east, tide turn & wind.
We hesitate on the brink of sinking, ourselves, to this cracked & heat-
hugged clay, to

                                      marsh gas the flicker of dead grass in water, swamp,
in all those small farms surrounded by ditches, road ditches, hand-
(gone, as ghost) dug ditches — "In those days drinking water was delivered
by wagon but they used ditch water for washing" their rags, now clay off
hands, translated by the tyee boss as anonymous numbers, "these men (who)
had to work 3 years to pay off their passage money" "were used by the
municipality to dig ditches." A pool of labour seeping into the land as

cannery workers, coolie gangs, saving to own some few acres of solid
ground

       despite the indestructible rot of vegetable matter, a mouldering
telephone book, somebody's clothing. Hands, it changes. Boughtup land,
sediment 10,000 feet of, wild clay furrows cracked in spring since 1968
no irrigation, this side of (the dyke) recurrent freshet, muddy & turbulent
(shaking of blue veins in a withered wrist

                     (not to be, NOT TO BE

in the dust, in the dust & dank of a boardedup house sun never lights
nor wind blows thru these windows dark against the day's heat lingering
still, as piss-fed grass this house is dead to, deaf the stalls of
adjoining barn a single pried door leads into

                        shadow bowls on a
broken chair, a solitary corner for someone's hurried mouthful gulped
by nightfallen fields already abandoned in prevision, the "last"
sunset, a "last" swallow soaring above the day's field, salvaged, tilled &
handpicked into fragile baskets of claydust, wrinkle eyes, sore back,
Looking up, under cornhusk & bambooslatted coolie hat at the monster
machine beating down the ditch, sucking, widening, raising the levee,
piledriver-&-dredge progress shoring familial fields their backs ache from,
their lives

                     (NOT TO BE TAKEN

For this was "flat prairie — good redtop grass," This was "swampy —
reeds, flags, low willows." A host of mosquitoes, dragonflies, small
crickets

       where no one stands

                empty, waiting the bulldozer tracts,
demolition, scaffolding & sewer drains, the ript denuded soil patches
of artificial grass will cover, like burial plots.

       "35 acres assembled & sold by Al Austin"

                                                            Afloat in a welter of
facts they left: Christmas cards in English from Chinese friends, Sunday
School biblical pictures, calendar, odd socks, receipts, broken crockery,
a blue bottle . . . a small hexagonal blue bottle with faded label, Chinese,
badly printed doctor's face. Uncorkt, a last lingering residue of some
red liquid, aromatic & strong as horse liniment.

                                                            This residue
faint as marsh gas over the soil, soiled, in blue raised letters down
one side, NOT TO BE TAKEN: a residue of pain, dug into the land.

Finn Road

"Seems like, with men around, you're always at the stove."
Making cabbage rolls, something that keeps in a slow oven when
the boys come back, late, from fishing. It's her day off. She
went to town to pay the bills, "somebody's got to look after that."
But tomorrow she'll be up when the tide's full, at 3 or 4 in the
morning, down to Finn Slough where her boat's moored. Been out
fishing for 20 years now. And walks, from counter to stove, with a
roll.

        It's a hot day, sultry, rain spit in the air.
There's cotton laid out on the kitchen table, a pattern. "Making
a housecoat," something cool to wear when it gets humid. Seems
like, whenever it's strawberry & haymaking time, there's rain.

A by-channel; a small backwater:

                        slough, Finn Slough (or Gilmour,
by Gilmour Island), slough for sale as "deep sea frontage,"
has been always, simply, backwater clutch of shacks, floats,
sheds: a swamp & dusty marsh grass sheltering mosquito boats,
small gillnetters & other vessels in this amphibious place,
half earth half water, half river half sea, tide fills, swiftly,
pushing muddy fingers into timbers of the float, crawling round
pilings & rushes, glinting up a web of net stranding float where
a man & woman bend, knotting holes deadheads & other refuse a murky
river roils, have torn, ripped, & otherwise scorned, sometimes from
leadline to cork . . .

                        The slow effort of
this people's morning: rise with predawn birdsong & coffee
stretching stiffer & stiffer bones, pack lunch, pad past the
cloistered silence of tv, crunch of gravel, drive (green Pinto)
down to where their boats lie, light filtering immense
vegetation.

                Check fuel, untie & start the engine ("a 7 Easthope
& a 15, wasn't it a 15 Easthope they had too? They thought they really

41

had something on the go — now when they look back they think it's a joke, you know, why, have we actually been fishing with those?"

"That was the onetime king engine" on this coast, days when nobody had any money, they bought a used car engine for two bucks, had it delivered down to the slough, the poor

                                shelter of swamp houses, float- ("when I look at it now it looks like a summer cabin") under the lee of a dyke Finnish squatters & other folk whose lives are inextricably tied with the tide that inundates their day, their time measured only by: this sucking at vegetal silence swallows shred, from the boom of idle boats, from the ridgepole of shadowy netshed jets drone: this land up for deep sea frontage ("oh yes, it'll be freighters & cement scow, barges & containerized shipping all the way up to New Westminister,

                              you can't stop progress, can you?"

                              How *accept* its creeping up? like a disease, like time, the tide they still know how to run, with it, up under ("remember how your net got wrapped & rolled?") that barge, danger at dark or fog, still after the fish which still run shadowy lines thru all that murk against the shifting bars of shipping channel, slipping that traffic, that bottom:

                                    "You sure find out when you get all the rubbish from down there — lot of bark, papers, bathroom papers — it's real messy sometimes. Trees & twigs & branches, branches of trees even floating down there. & then there's, I dunno what kind of plant it is, it's like a crabapple limb & it's just full of little twigs, & that's a wicked one when it gets caught in to a thin net. & ends of logs that have been cut, you know, stump ends & round blocks drifting. The sawmills open their gates, you know, & let all their loose stuff out — when that comes dashing there's even sawdust in the river."

At bottom of this slippery time, it's her boat,
her feet on, managing the freshet, swollen, flooding (highest tides
of the year last week) water on water swell, with a wind running
norwesterly "it gets pretty choppy here," "I've been here with a blow
that's bin blowing 47 miles an hour — just big big waves washing
way up above the rocks." "See it's narrow & when the wind blows
those waves break & cross, it gets *real* rough."

She runs in the
throat of time, voicing the very swifts & shallows of that river,
urging, in the dash of it, enough to keep up, to live on. When nets
are up 50%, fuel's up, & the packer's taking chum salmon, undressed,
at 20 cents a pound, "the same they sell in the stores dressed at $1.20,
while they're selling the roe they don't even pay us for at $2.20
a pound, clear profit" . . .

Somehow they survive the oily waters swirling
under packers piling, bargeloads of herring sucked up, truckloads
left to rot, salmon on ice in the packerboats collecting twenty hours
a day,

Somehow they survive, this people, these fish,
survive the refuse bottom, filthy water, their choked lives,
in a singular dance of survival, each from each. At the
narrows, in the pressure of waves so checked & held by
"deep-sea frontage" it's the river's push against her, play of
elements her life comes rolling on. Hair flying, in gumboots,
on deck with rubber apron ("it's no dance dress"), she'll take
all that river gives, willing only to stand her ground (rolling,
with it, right under her feet, her life, rolling, out from under,
right on out to sea . . .

Response

"I think the fish like their water clean too,"
she says, with a dry laugh where: this outgoing
river, this incoming tide

                              mingle & meet. To take
no more than the requisite, *required* to grow, spawn,
catch, die: required to eat.

Intelligence (as if by radio?

Moon river rising, raising a
ghost, Intensifies its run of living water (wind riffle
cold tonight) against this black, these mat pilings, solid as
deadheads, eaten away by time.

Light temporary (occasional cloud &,
she's moving west, as always, with our spin away from, knots of,
black chunks of history (old cannery pilings, old sheds rotting their
legs into the rapid run of water westward, to the sun's going,
to the open rising of the wind, easterly, betrays rain . . . Full moon
one night in twenty-eight. Full moon minus rain one time in nine
of that, or thereabouts,

Night, I'm wanting to catch you *this* time
(the moon's unwinding burial blanket, time, stands in its warp
temporarily only, light —

Legs of, sheds, stumps, amputated limbs
(torn knots nets are, shadows only. Where's the *body* of this being
we run against? & feel, this net we're caught in, fish, light on
full, suddenly blinded in its extent:

This black & white we only half perceive is caught by a wave-
photography moon operates on a full night, quiet, most of the boats
out. Wave reading shed, telegraphy of pilings in the river's
intimate creak of hulls shatter — a dog bark somewhere, the sudden
chuckle of sea, someone scratching his head, turns in with the last
bilge into creeping water, splash. This continues . . .

                        & if the mono-
chrome of white & red, the sloping roofs of Canadian Fish resemble,
light in the moon like old siding Chinese backs rest beside, a pipe,
a break in the sun from soldering work — some cannery with its
clanking stream of cans, its steam, its rot of excessive fish
still on the dock of *that* time

                   if, behind the dyke (tracks),
there's a ghostly clutter of Indian tenement/ Japanese cannery shacks
whose "floor . . . is littered with blankets, furniture, cooking tins,
fish gear, carnival masks, & usually 3 or 4 dogs" while "over the
doorway is a board with L1356 or whatever happens to be the number
of the boat in which the man goes out to meet the salmon coming in"
and when "a boat is found bottom up, its number is taken & the
inhabitants of that shack are notified"

                  & if there is still,
further along, under the gravel of cannery parking lot, a picket
fence, a woman's wailing all night long, for what? for what return
the present *doesn't* ride upon? It's not linear:

                  the stainless
steel lines going down in the Gulf echo other trollings, catch
in the mesh of a net we refuse to see, the accretion of all our
actions, how they interact, how they inter/read (intelligence),
receive, the reading the sea, a vanishing marsh, a dying river,
the mesh we are netted in, makes of *us*.

Life Cycle

"after spawning they are exhausted, greatly
emaciated, & soon die, their bodies sinking
to the bed of the stream or lodging in the
drift at its side."

Flakes, flakes of fire, fish flakes. Or flaked out after the last
shift, flakey chips & salt grains on the tables of the Steveston,
beer going down cool & easy in the light, settling down into a
round chair, friends playing shuffleboard, chatting in the long
low hall, no wind.

                      Outside, flakes of moonlight on the
black river. Outside reeks of fish, like it always has. "Today
we cook at Holly, Harlock & Wellington," (1894). After the flood
"it's been a hard pull, but I think it's safe now with more
piling."

          Safe against that river cresting at over 20 feet.
Safe again, forgetting she's a way in, to return, in time, the
stream. Against all odds they home in, to the source that's
marked their scales first birth place: environing:

                                                    It rings us
where we are (turn & turn about), however the depth   its cool
waters glide (over us), erase, with vast space elide the code
we've managed to forget: this urge to return, & returning, thresh,
in those shallows, death, leaving what slips by, the spore,
the spawn, the mark that carries on . . . like a germ, like violence
in the flesh,

             as if, hooknosed, holding to the shape they burn in,
salmon don't re-enter time (in four years, the river), or,

In the long low hall where lights inexplicably darken & exhaust
their fire (& the canneries with long blackout drapes, the crepe,
the pall not elsewhere, over the Pacific, but here: "you wouldn't
want to go outside . . ."

                             as if the earth were dead
& we within it ash, eating ash, drinking the lead fire of our own
consumption, "Here's to us!"

                    As if, "outside," a white fire *doesn't*
ring us, earth flicker its own circuits we, transparent, burn within.

Sun & Moon thru the Japanese Fishermen's Hospital (1898–1942)

Up the stairs; up the stairs, wild geese outside, wind blows thru your
hair, thru delta, marsh grass (up the stairs' silt, thick with it
hot with this *sun* that burns up off the sea / earth

                                        (hibiscus?

                                                            Up the
stairs it says Japanese Fishermen's Hospital, weathered, & the plank
siding, planks we climb up (the stairs: there is no way I can avoid
looking your look as you turn:

                                        wharf, boat, yard arms
& the moon glimmering its strange eye down river, down where the
mouth is.

        I've known you a long time, I've known you in this marshy
selvedge (thick with the rim of the earth's shadow turning, into sun.

        I've known this estuary light filled, Garry Light (its mouth
whose strands run wet with water sinking into white, barred, light.

        I've seen your hand on the weathered planking *this*
side of the hospital we climb, *against* the sun & into shadow, wait:
where blurred faces tranquil lie, afternoon sand across the wooden

floor, the nurse, this person dying or giving birth? a single red
hibiscus fading, into its glass.

We've come to where, what, changes at the heart: this General
Ward, white a, widow's mouth (sea glinting just offshore), a
mother's hole? We've come to generations, generation, Steveston,
at the heart: our death is gathering (salmon) just offshore, as,
back there in this ghostly place we have (somehow) entered (where?)
you turn & rise, gently, into me.

Ghost

oily ring shimmering, scintillating round the stern
of the boat you have just painted, *Elma K,* all your ties to shore,
your daughters, wife. Candy cache for the littlest grandchild
peering, short-frocked, over the pen where you, below water level,
fork up out of the deep — hooked, iced, dressed in slimey
death rendered visible — salmon.

"Nobody talks about them
anymore," the ghosts that used to rise when you, a child, crossing
the dyke from BC Packers, night, saw, Out of the dark this strange
white light, or covering someone's rooftop, invisible to all but
strangers, this blue light telling of death.

(methane? invisible organic rot? We only know the extinction
of open marsh by concrete; the burial of burial ground by corporate
property.

But *then* there were places, you say, Chinaman's Hat,
where you couldn't sleep at night, fresh flower in your cabin, for
the host of restless souls' unburied hands outstretcht, returning,
claim their link with the decomposing earth

(ancestral: fertile as
death: hello briar rose, blackberry & trumpet flower. All their faces
lucent & warmlipt shining before your eyes: teachers, cabaret girls,
longlegged American army wives you chauffeured, cared for, daughters,
friends of your daughters, down thru the water smiles of easy girls,
caught, kore, in the black hole of your eye, yourself a ghost now
of the natural world.

Were you fined? Did you cross the border inad-
vertently? Did chart & compass, all direction, fail? Interned,
your people confined to a small space where rebirth, will,
push you out thru rings of material prosperity at war's
end fixed, finally, as citizens of an exploited earth:
you drive your own car, construct your own house, create your
registered place at Packers' camp, walk the fine (concrete)
line of private property.

But still, at night, tied up in some dark harbour,
it's the cries of women in orgasm you hear echoing, with the slap of
water against your hull, coming in, coming in, from far reaches
of the infinite world. And still, at sea, boundaries give way:
white women, white bellies of salmon thieved by powerful boats.

There are no territories. And the ghosts of landlocked camps are
all behind you. Only the blip of depth sounder & fish finder,
harmonic of bells warning a taut line, & the endless hand over
hand flip of the fish into silver pen — successive, infinite —

What do the charts say? Return, return. Return of what doesn't
die. Violence in mute form. Walking a fine line.

Only, always to dream of erotic ghosts of the flowering earth;
to return to a decomposed ground choked by refuse, profit, & the
concrete of private property; to find yourself disinherited from
your claim to the earth.

Or there is love

we'd house ourselves in, all this wind & rain.
Confuse us. Driving lines that shift, the floor does, ground or
under sea, to cast, at low tide what lies uncaught, uncovered
traces only, of sun & the moon's pull.

Unseen, how lines run
from place to place, How driving from town she follows the water's
push, the fields, drained by ditch to river to, the sea at,
where she lives . . . "At the end of the road," she says
Steveston is. At the mouth, where river runs under, in, to the
immanence of things.

To live in a place. Immanent. In
place. Yet to feel at sea. To come from elsewhere & then to discover
love, has a house & name. Has land. Is landed, under the swaying
trees which bend, so much in this wind like underwater weeds we think
self rises from.

But the place itself, mapt out, a web, was grass:
tall, bent grass swaying heavy with seed. Cottonwood whose
seeds make a web in the wind. "It was a wild place — where foxes

might live," this marsh persistent bending windswept lines of force,
current, men drag their nets thru to recover (as if they could)
wealth

       (fishy as quick slime, saying, it's here, & here, & here,
this self

         whose wealth consists of what?

                            A house? built by
hands & handed down from father to not son but daughter, tenuous as
moonlight sometimes, hair so strong sun weaves ladders in it, webs,
of strange connection. Light & dark. And so from this place to
center, dreaming of the source of things, flow, a ditch, from there to
. . . Japan & back? No, somehow love runs, shaken by the waters' pull
& leaves a network of men beached, Remembering now whose name,
in the dark the one owl calls & foxes' gloaming eyes, lit up by
the future (moon) say love, love will be . . . a fisherman's dream,
the web, the snare . . .

To retain, to remember, simply, the right names for things. Kneeling
by the bed, in a knotting of grass she seeks to see her life (oinari-san,
by the power of foxes) dreams: I found myself in a hall piled high with
dirty dishes, no one around, I had to wash them all. How they pile up,
these leftovers trapt, out of the flow. Like the fish. Like the
network of fishy familial parts these knots are, "my daughter, my house,"
these knots that bind.

         At the end of the road, at the river's mouth,
muddy with all these empty dykes & misplaced hope, she's removed herself,
disappearing like foxes of the past into the underbrush, whose wall's
this briar hall of moonlight, whisper of old rituals: who are you now
you've cut yourself adrift, alone?

             "I'm not really in
the Japanese community, I don't belong to Buddhist Church, I don't
send my kids to sunday school."

Who also, neither north or south, drives back, late, by the shining
watery roads from town, from the Western Front, from the center of things,
to mud & drainage ditch, familiar house, shit, the accumulation of
personal things. To the place of firstcomers where a woman felt
"like I was living in a wild field," where the grass, where the lines of
wind, where the lines of power moved clear in a field of power.

                                         Where now her house stands
webbed with weaving, leaf tracery & light (of pots, plants), a house she
inhabits, immanent, at the edge of town a field they're raising houses on.
And coming from town, driving down by the scummy & soontobecovered ditches
(remnant, of leftover rains, plucked cabbages in the sun, & wind) where do you
find her, out?

            as now by day,

                          or in, summer's wilder growth, around &
past (the stepping stones at back are wood & cut by hand) amidst (there is
no closer) hands full of beans & fingers in the heart of, "well I *live* here,"
lettuce, children, friends, you find a self, under the trees that sway like
underwater weeds, connecting things.

Steveston, B.C.

Steveston: delta, mouth of the Fraser where the river empties, sandbank after sandbank, into a muddy Gulf.

Steveston: onetime cannery boomtown: "salmon capital of the world": fortunes made & lost on the homing instinct of salmon.

Steveston: home to 2,000 Japanese, "slaves of the company": stript of all their belongings, sent to camps in the interior away from the sea, wartime, who gradually drift back in the '40's, few who even buy back their old homes, at inflated prices, now owning modern ranchstyle etc, & their wives, working the cannery, have seniority now, located.

Steveston: hometown still for some, a story: of belonging (or is it continuing? lost, over & over . . .

Steveston divided into lots with an ox barbecue, sold the lot but only bit by bit Steveston belongs to its temporal landowners & those who, Packers & Nelson Brothers, Canadian Fish, hold chunks of the waterfront like gaps (teeth) of private territory, "use at your own risk," but the shark (with his teeth dear) speculates, brooding on housing developments whose sidewalks pave over the dyke, whose street lamps obliterate the shadow bowl of night on Lum Poy's field, west, & south, as the geese fly past the old Steves place & on, to dark to

                                                            wherever fish come from, circling back in
to their source:

                        We obscure it with what we pour on these waters, fuel, paint, fill,
the feeding line linking us to Japan & back, wherever, cargo ships, freighters
steam up river & only the backwaters house these small boats whose owners,
displaced & now relocated as fishermen can be, fishing up nets full of shadow/
food for the canneries to pack, blip blip sonar & even these underwater
migrations visible now as routes, roots, the river roots, out from under

                                                                        brail net

they lift these fishes with, reading a river gulf, Or, visibly

how it pours, this river, right over the top of the rock dam into Cannery Channel
swirling freshet on & right on past the sedge that roots sediment, witness these
gaptoothed monument pilings, pile stumps of ghostly canneries settle, into
obscurity (a map necessary, or key, to the old locations) locating thus
(where are we?) shipwreck, a rusty wheel, a drum, inarticulate emblems of
this life craft that runs, that continues, this busy work of upkeep (*without
us*) wheeling its river bank into sun, into the blind anonymity of sea light,
the open

              sun. a sea men sink their lives into, continue, dazzlingly undeciphered,
unread days, dazed with the simple continuance of water pour, of wind, of small
stores turning their annual credit ledgers, debit, silent as winter falls, falls,
pours.

                        This is the story of a town, these are the people, whose
history locates inside of dream, in site of (in situ) down by the riverbank a
torrent pouring past its sloughs & back channels, boat basins time repeats, this
one was Phoenix, this one Atlas, or leaving Hong Wong/Wo's obliterated letters,
even whole names along with bits of crockery water washes, dead dogs, web caught
up under the shadows of these buildings men would cast, like nets of retrieval,
only to cast their names across the line that water washes, away, incessant,
swollen, by reaches of the sea our lives respond to, irresistibly drawn, these
precarious floats, boats equipt with the latest machinery, radar, sonic scan,

drifting, limbs extended, sometimes logs & deadheads, sometime creatures of motive that swim, *against* the source, but always continuing to return, always these lovely & perilous bodies drifting in spawn, swarm on out to sea.

generation, generations at the mouth

clans of salmon, chinook, coho, gathering just off shore, backbones no longer
intact, steam-pressured in millions of cans, picked clean barbecue leavings in a
thousand garbage bags ripped open by cats, rats, they can't find their way back

what is the body's blueprint?

return what is solid to water, the first peoples said —
returned, every bone intact
generates the giving back of race, kind, kin

choked in urban outfalls, fished as they aim for rivers sediment-thick with run-
off, *tamahnous* of the wild they hover, sonar streaks, impossible vision-glitches,
outside pens where farmed lookalikes grow pale & drugged

kin, wild skin, wild & electric at the mouth where rivers disappear in the that
that is not that, the chinook can't find their way back

come out of the blue: this flow, these energy rivers & wheels, radiant giving
unlocked. & not this frozen, this canned product eagles once stripped, eagles,
bears going, gone, hungry & wild outside shut doors where light pools & we
pore over stock market news, refuse, refuse our interrelation, refuse to pour
back

what *is* the body's blueprint? impermanent, shifting energy blocks in its own
becoming, a stream & streaming out to the void where rivers lose themselves

in the bardo as many beings as waves gather at any opening, those in-between
and not-yet ones that race a river of sperm to be here now, light-pour, each cell
in its dying turn returns

what is the mouth of the river now? a toxic O of emptiness? teeming hole of
ever-becoming we create? re-entry. re-turn. verbing the noun out of its stuck
edges and into occurrence, currents, *curre-* . . . we've lost the verb in our
currency, a frozen exchange streaming emptiness

(they're fishing in London now)

at the mouth of the river, clans of the possible are gathering, the chinook,
the coho rivering just offshore are us

— January 2000

The Steveston Photographs

Hideo (Henry) Kokubo, fisherman, 1974

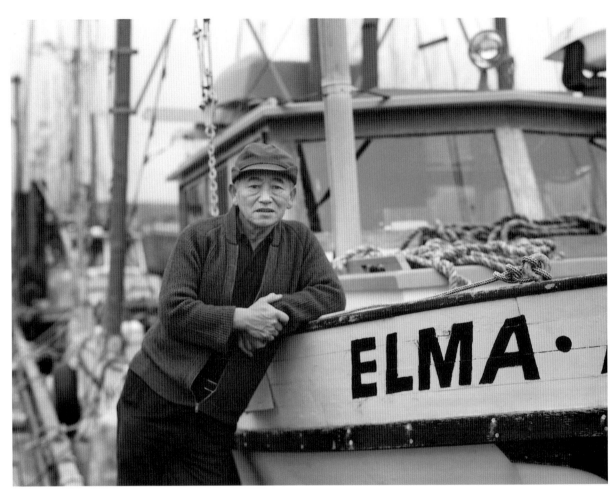

Hideo Kokubo with his boat, ELMA•K, 1974

Gillnetter, Star Camp, 1974

Canadian Pacific Camp, spring 1973

Fisherman, 1973

Old Cannery Buildings, Cannery Way, 1974

Ship Builder, Britannia Shipyards, 1974

Fisherman, Canadian Pacific Camp, 1974

"Children Keep Out," net shed, 1973

Herring, 1974

Cannery Workers, 1974

Cannery Workers, B.C. Packers, 1973

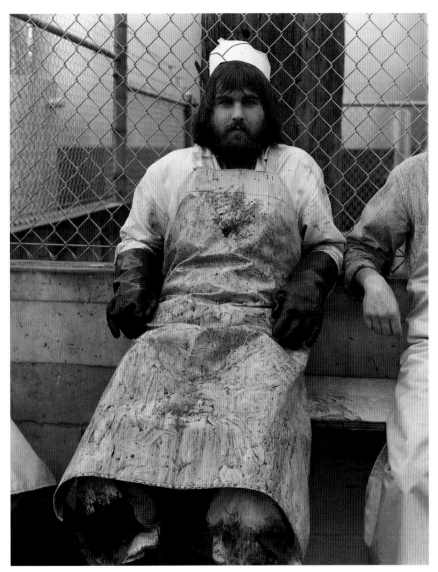

Cannery Workers, B.C. Packers, 1973

Finn Slough, October 1974

Gill Net, 1973

Inez Huovinen, fisherwoman, Finn Slough, 1973

Charlie Huovinen, mending net, Finn Slough, 1973

Crossing Moncton Street, 1973

Steveston Barbers, Moncton Street, 1974

Pool Hall, Moncton Street, 1973

Christine's Café, Moncton Street, 1974

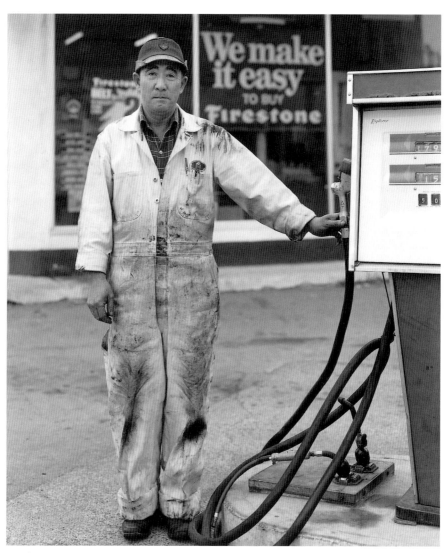

Worker, Marine Garage, Moncton Street, 1973

Worker, Marine Garage, Moncton Street, 1974

Woman and Boy Outside the Ship 'n Shore Hair Stylist, Moncton Street, 1973

Hair Stylists, a few moments later, 1973

The Librarian, Steveston Library, 1973

Boy, Moncton Street, 1973

Three Women, New Denver, June 1973

Ryuichi and Kimi Yoshida, outside their house, New Denver, 1973

Rintaro Hayashi, kendo teacher, 1973

Moto Suzuki, retired cannery worker, seated in her home, 1975

Hideo (Henry) Kokubo, 1973

Tsuneko (Koko), artist, Hideo Kokubo's daughter, 1973

Tsuneko and Her Children, Aaron and Gen, 1974

Tsuneko and Her Children, a few moments later, 1974

Eiko Kokubo, 1974

Aaron, 1974

Three Boys, Moncton Street, 1973

Three Brothers, Number Two Road, 1974

Moto Suzuki, 1975

Farm, Number One Road, Spring 1974

Old Couple, 1974

Afterword

Looking at photographs through the prism of years, different eyes than a quarter of a century ago . . . the stories and faces flood my memory. And I remember us then, Daphne and I, passionate about our exploration of Steveston, still stirred with that wondrous naiveté born of North American humanism and idealism that swept us into the 1960s and beyond. It mattered. The stories mattered. Getting it right, mattered. "Seeking to perceive it as it stands . . ." A certain cadence. Is it even possible to be so enraptured again? We talked and argued sharing a commitment to our disciplines that both separated and joined us. We were always two. Two voices, two perspectives, and we presented the ideas, the "findings" in two distinct yet overlapping folios, the words and the pictures.

The photographs made then, at that time, in that fishing village that I visited for the first time, was my introduction to the Japanese-Canadian experience of dislocation and displacement. Stories took me to New Denver, one of the sites of forced resettlement during the war years. Included as a fragment of the telling are two of the images made from there.

At the mouth of the Fraser river I remember a slow dance of meeting, listening and photographing. I see myself with my large wooden camera on tripod, black focusing cloth flailing out and over me . . . photography as street theatre, photographing as focusing.

Then, the "veracity" of the photograph, like the mesh of the gill net, entangled us.

— Robert Minden
August 2000, Vancouver

107

Steveston Photographs 1973–1975

Notes on the Poems

PAGE 37: *Not to be taken*
material quoted in this poem from the Richmond Art Center's oral history files —
interviews with William Gilmore and Les Gilmore.

PAGE 41: *A by-channel; a small backwater*
quoted material thanks to Inez Huovinen.

PAGE 45: *Intelligence*
quoted material from "Steveston-by-the-Fraser," Garnett Weston, *British Columbia Magazine,*
August 1911.

PAGE 47: *Life Cycle*
opening paragraph quoted from Dr. J.P. Babcock's treatise on Pacific salmon in Appendix 3
of Cicely Lyons' book, *Salmon: Our Heritage,* B.C. Packers Ltd., 1969. Other material in
this poem quoted from the same book.

Notes on the Photographs

I photographed in Steveston using a large wooden camera on a tripod, a 5 x 7 Deardorf with
reducing back to yield 4 x 5 negatives. For this edition, I considered all of the negatives made
during 1973, 1974 and 1975. Some, that I had never printed, previously dismissing them while
paying homage to a more formal aesthetic, now seem compelling. Others I had printed differently
than I would print today. This edition includes nine photographs that were not included in earlier
editions, and four others that have been reprinted, opened up to their full negative. These new prints
were made by Trevor Martin, a dedicated photographic printer faithful to the silver image. The rest
of the reproductions are from vintage gelatin-silver prints that I made in the early 1970s.

PAGE 73: *"Children Keep Out," net shed, 1973*
This writing on a door to a net shed, addressed to the young, was freshly painted in 1973. It uses
Kanji and Katakana characters together, a writing style particular to pre-World War Two Japan.

Daphne Marlatt, who has spent most of her life living and writing on the West Coast, has played an important part in creating an alternative poetic line. Her previous poetry titles include *Salvage*, *Ghost Works*, *Touch to My Tongue*, and *How Hug a Stone*. She has also published two novels: *Taken* and *Ana Historic*. She now makes her home in Vancouver.

Robert Minden is a photographer, story-teller and composer. After teaching sociology at several universities, Minden turned to the still camera for a more intuitive inquiry. The *Steveston* photographs soon followed. He is currently working on a photographic portrait of artists while continuing his contemporary journey in experimental music. He lives in Vancouver.